AF886675

How To Make Money Online with Affiliate marketing

Legal Information

Copyright Information:

DISCLAIMER/LEGAL NOTICES:

ISBN: 978-0-9964087-2-1

No Liability:

Table of Contents

ISBN: 978-0-9964087-2-1

Introduction

Thanks for purchasing this Book. You now have everything you need in order to be able to start your own successful affiliate marketing business. This Book is going to explain and expose you to a very lucrative business model that you can use to begin making money online. If you've tried and failed at making money online before, don't worry, this book covers everything A to Z and gives you the complete picture you need to be able to start your own affiliate marketing business.

What Affiliate Marketing Is

In order to be successful at affiliate marketing we need to understand the business model completely. So let's go over what affiliate marketing is and how you can use it to make money. Affiliate marketing always starts with product vendors. There are all types of business owners and companies out there who have products for sale over the Internet.

These products can be anything ranging from e-books, DVDs, to actual physical products that are shipped to customers doors. Because the Internet is such a huge place and the product owner cannot hope to reach his entire audience by himself, he enlists the help of affiliates.

Affiliates go out and use various Internet marketing techniques to find people to buy the products. They then refer the customer over to the product vendor where they purchase the product. Once this happens, the product vendor credits the affiliate with a sale and gives him a percentage of the profits. This is referred to as earning commissions.

ISBN: 978-0-9964087-2-1

Why You Should Consider Affiliate Marketing for Income

Affiliate marketing is a great business model for anyone interested in making money on the Internet. I says great for several reasons. First, it's relatively easy to do. You don't need a lot of technical skill or computer ability in order to be able to make money with affiliate marketing.

The second reason why like affiliate marketing is a business model is because you don't have to worry about inventory or customer service. As an affiliate you're only responsibility is to refer customers to the product vendor in order to make sales. It is the product vendor's responsibility to handle inventory, ship out products, and deal with customer support.

Finally with affiliate marketing you get paid on time every time if you work with a large affiliate network. In other online business models you have to worry about when you're going to get access to your money. With affiliate marketing, if you're working with the network, you receive your income checks on a weekly or biweekly basis no questions asked.

So with these reasons in mind is pretty obvious why affiliate marketing can be one of the most lucrative business activities that you can do online. Sorry eager to get started making money with affiliate marketing? If so let's go on and dive deeper into this amazing business model.

ISBN: 978-0-9964087-2-1

System Overview

In this book we are going to cover a simple system that anyone can use to make money with affiliate marketing. Before we break down the system and going to each component in-depth, you need to know how everything fits together so you can get the big picture.

The system starts with picking good niche market that has affiliate products that you can promote. Market research is absolutely critical to the success of the system. If you build your affiliate marketing business in a market that isn't so good, you going to put a ceiling on the level of success you can experience. However, if you choose a good niche market to build your business in, you can literally make thousands are hundreds of thousands of dollars in profit.

After you've chosen your market the next step is going to be creating an informational blog for that marketplace. The reason we do this is because the Internet is the information superhighway. People most often come online seeking information about a subject. If these people can find our blog, we have an opportunity to sell affiliate products. Which leads us right into the next step...

After creating an informational blog we're going to find and recommend related affiliate products to our blog visitors. Because people are looking for information on our particular subject, they will be more likely to buy products related to that subject. So here's how it all works in a nutshell...

A person hits the Internet looking for information about a particular niche market. They use a search engine or look on other websites for this information. Due to our marketing efforts they find links linking back to our website. They visit our website,

ISBN: 978-0-9964087-2-1

which is an informational blog, and there able to read high-quality content related to the information they were looking for.

While they are there, we recommend them affiliate products that are related to the niche market in question. When they purchase these affiliate products we make money. The cycle repeats over and over again, and we make more and more money. So let's get started with how you do this…

ISBN: 978-0-9964087-2-1

Step One: Picking a Niche

The very first step of the process is choosing a niche market. Your niche market selection is vitally important to the success of your affiliate marketing business. A great affiliate marketing business set up in a bad niche market won't make nearly as much money as a mediocre affiliate business set up in a great niche market. So you're going to want to make sure that you choose a niche market that is going to be profitable for affiliate marketing.

What Makes a Profitable Niche Market

We're going to be using informational blogs as the basis for our affiliate marketing business so were going to need an information-based niche market in order to be able to ensure ourselves the most success. Information-based niche markets are markets where people regularly access the Internet looking for information related to those niche markets.

If people aren't regularly coming online looking for information, then we won't have very many customers that we can sell affiliate products to. In order to come up with of great profitable information-based niche market you should ask yourself several questions:

Does the niche market have magazines and books?

If there are companies that are actively publishing books and magazines inside of niche market that indicates that their customers and people actively consuming information inside of that niche. This is a great sign for affiliate marketing because essentially will be going after those same customers.

ISBN: 978-0-9964087-2-1

Does the niche market have other websites?

If there are other webmasters and marketers out there online with websites inside of this niche market that means there is money to be made in the marketplace. In this case competition is a good sign, so use Google to search for other blogs and websites inside of the market you're considering.

Do the people interested in the niche market have disposable income?

You want to make sure that the people inside the niche market have disposable income that they can spend on products and services related to the niche. If you're trying to sell products and services to a of people you have a hard time making money. However, if your customers have disposable income that they can spend on products you'll find it relatively easy to earn money.

Are the people interested in the niche market used to shopping online?

You also want to make sure that the people interested in the niche market are used to find things over the Internet. You can ask yourself is the average person in this niche tech savvy enough to want to buy things online? You need to know this information before you get started because you're only going to be selling over the Internet, and if people have buying resistance to shopping that way you'll find hard to make money.

Are the people interested in the niche market desperate for information or solutions to problems?

Lastly you want to know if the people interested in the niche market have problems that they are trying to solve, are there desperate for information. Problems in desperation give your customers a drive to want to purchase products that offer them

ISBN:_978-0-9964087-2-1

solutions and give them information to help them reach their goals are meet their needs. If you can find a niche with desperation and problems driving people online looking for answers you can rest assure that there's a lot of money to be made for you.

So, if you can answer yes to all of these questions then you've discovered a very profitable niche market that you can make a lot of money and as an affiliate. In order to get you started coming up with some great niche markets here is a list of some of the top profitable niche markets online for affiliate marketing:

Hobbies

Hobby niche markets are great marketplace is because people simply love their hobbies. They will spend an exorbitant amount of time, energy, and even money to involve themselves with their hobbies. They will purchase not one, but multiple products are related to the hobbies and gladly spend money. If you can get your hands on some of this free-flowing money you can become really successful as an affiliate marketer inside of a hobby niche.

Weight Loss

There many people all over the world who are overweight and want to lose weight. However, due to the nature of the weight loss industry there is a ton of different type of information out there about how to lose weight properly. This means there are literally millions of people online searching for weight loss information at any given moment. If you can tap into this wellspring of website visitors and put them in front of a great affiliate product you can make a lot of money.

ISBN: 978-0-9964087-2-1

Make More Money

People all over the world want to make more money. It doesn't matter who you are or how much money you have, you can always use more money. This is why make more money products like Internet marketing, stock market, foreign exchange currency trading, real estate, and other investment type products sell well. If you can get in affiliate business establish inside of this niche market you can make a lot of money too.

Relationships

Relationships are universal human experience. People are the that looking to get into relationships, trying to save their current relationship, or even get married. This means that thousands and even millions of people come online everyday looking for advice related to relationships. If you can create informational blog about relationships and get some of this web traffic, you can recommend relationship related affiliate products and make a ton of money in the process.

You can use one of these niche markets, are use the questions above to come up with your own profitable niche markets. Either way, what you discovered the great niche market you going to want to move on to the next step...

ISBN:_978-0-9964087-2-1

Step Two: Find Affiliate Products To Promote

After you've chosen the niche market to build your affiliate marketing business in, the next step is to find actual products that you can promote to that marketplace. Now there are two different types of affiliate marketing products that you have to be concerned about when looking for affiliate products to promote.

Digital Products

Digital affiliate marketing products are products that are able to be digitally downloaded onto the customer's computer right after purchase. These products can be e-books, reports, software, audio courses, and even video courses. These products have high profit margins since it is completely free to reproduce a digital product.

With these high profit margins come high commissions, has figures are willing to reward affiliates much more of the profit since it's so easy to reproduce the product. Digital Products are great for the type of affiliate marketing were going to be doing, because their information-based products. Since we're creating in informational blog inside of an information-based niche, it is natural to sell information-based products to our customers.

Physical Products

Physical affiliate marketing products are products that have to be shipped out to the customer's home or office in order for them to use them. These types of products can be anything physical that a person can actually feel in touch. These products have very small profit margins which means affiliate commissions won't be that high.

ISBN: 978-0-9964087-2-1

However, many affiliates find it easier to sell physical products as opposed to Digital Products because people know exactly what they're going to be receiving the order physical product. With a digital product the person is left in the dark until they actually purchase the product. This means you have to overcome much more buying resistance when you're selling a digital product as opposed to physical product.

In order to make a lot of money selling physical products as an affiliate you are going sell a lot of them in volume. This can be done relatively easy as long as you pick the right niche.

Finding Affiliate Products

so how do we go about finding affiliate products to sell? Well, the first place to start is the top affiliate marketing networks. These networks are places where product vendors can attract sellers to promote their products. Let's talk about the biggest affiliate networks:

Become a JVZoo Affiliate

It is free to become an affiliate at JVZoo. You will have instant access to all of our affiliate tools and training.

Http://jvzoo.com

Clickbank (digital only products)

Clickbank is the world's leading marketplace for digital downloadable products. They literally have 100,000 or more Digital Products available for download. As an affiliate you can promote any one of these products and enjoy a healthy commissions anywhere from 25% on up to 75% of the sale price. Because most Clickbank products sell between $17 and $97 you can end up making a lot of money with relatively few sales.

ISBN: 978-0-9964087-2-1

Here's a link to the Clickbank marketplace:

http://www.Clickbank.com

Amazon (mostly physical products)

Amazon.com started as the Internet's number one book retailer, but they quickly expanded out to become one of the top online retailers in the entire world. Amazon literally has means of products available on this marketplace, and most of them are physical products. You can join Amazon is an affiliate and sell any one of these products and enjoy commissions between 4% and 8%.

That may not seem like a lot, but Amazon has set up his website so that people tend to order multiple products at one time and they may even buy products that you didn't even recommend to them. The end result is that you can sell a lot of Amazon product volume, which quickly adds up to a lot of money. Depending on your niche market you may want to consider Amazon as your source for products.

Here's the link to the Amazon affiliate program:

http://affiliate-program.amazon.com

Commission Junction (physical and Digital Products)

Commission Junction is another great affiliate marketplace. There are some really big brands there that have both physical and Digital Products available for you to earn commissions on. If you're looking for affiliate products to promoting your business you should definitely stop by their website and check them out.

Here's a link to the Commission Junction affiliate program:

http://www.cj.com/

ISBN: 978-0-9964087-2-1

other smaller affiliate marketplaces (physical and Digital Products)

there are also other great affiliate marketplace networks out there that you should search in order to find great affiliate products to promote for your affiliate business. Here's a list of some of my favorite affiliate marketing networks besides the big three that I've already mentioned:

http://www.linkshare.com/

https://www.shareasale.com/

http://www.avantlink.com/

http://www.pepperjamnetwork.com/

https://ebaypartnernetwork.com/files/hub/en-US/index.html

http://peerfly.com/

http://clicksure.com/

After you've search to these networks and found a few products that you like to promote is an affiliate is time to move on to the next step...

ISBN: 978-0-9964087-2-1

Step Three: Creating Your Blog

The next step in the process is to get your informational blog website up and running on the Internet. This blog is going to be the hub of your affiliate marketing business. People will find your blog do to your marketing efforts, and once there you going to treat them to some high-quality content related to the subject they were searching for. So let's get started…

Picking a Good Domain Name

the first thing you need to do before creating a website is, with a good domain name that you can brand your site with. The best types of domain names to get are .com domain names, but.net's, .org's, and .info domain names can work well to.

My favorite place to register domain names is

http://domainsandprofit.com

http://godaddy.com

http://www.namecheap.com

Once on that website you can use the simple search bar to find domain names that are available, and once you find one that you like you can register it.

ISBN: 978-0-9964087-2-1

A good domain name needs to have the following qualities:

Pronounceable

Your domain name should be pronounceable. A non-pronounceable domain name is hard to use for an affiliate marketing business because people have a hard time saying the domain name. You want your domain name to be made of real words, or use words that don't necessarily mean anything, but that people can pronounce.

Memorable

A good domain name is also memorable. It's usually short and made up of one or two words. A long domain name is going to be hard to remember, and if people can't remember your domain name it is unlikely they will visit your website.

Brandable

A good domain name is also brandable. This means that you can build a brand based on your domain name. An example of this is Skype. The word Skype is a necessarily mean anything, but it's a brandable word so they have branded instant messaging technology to that name. Now what people say "Skype me" everyone knows what they mean.

Keep these tips in mind when choosing a domain name for your affiliate marketing business and you can rest assure that the domain you choose is going to be a good one.

ISBN: 978-0-9964087-2-1

the best software to use to run your website with is Wordpress. WordPress is completely free blog software, and many consider it the most powerful blog software out there. After you've got your domain name you going to need to add to domain into your web host. Once you've done that, it's time to install WordPress.

You can also create wordpress blog/site from your hosting cpanel. Most of cpanel has "wordpress" icon or "fantastico" icon. Loginto to your cpanel and click on that icon and follow the instructions.

If you are not technically oriented you can higher someone from fiver.com for $5 to create your blog.

If you've never installed WordPress before here's a short tutorial that shows you how to do it:

http://www.siteground.com/tutorials/wordpress/wordpress-installation.htm

After you do this you should have the default installation of WordPress on your website. The next step is to choose an appropriate theme for your website. The WordPress themes like the design of your website and changing to a new theme can totally change the look of your website.

Here's a list of the best places to find free WordPress themes that you can install on your WordPress website:

http://www.wplocker.com

http://www.fwpthemes.com

http://fthe.me/wordpress-themes/free/

http://www.fabthemes.com/

http://wordpress.org/themes/

ISBN: 978-0-9964087-2-1

After choosing your theme, the next thing you need to do is plan out and create your actual content.

Planning and Creating Your Website Content

Since you're running an informational blog, you're going to want to update it constantly with content related to your niche market. This type of content is going to be informative high-quality blog posts that provide people who are coming to your site with great information. So let's use an example niche set as you can see how to plan out a website's content.

For this example let's use the weight loss niche. Now, the ultimate goal of your website is to become the premier go to place raw information related to your niche market. So in this case you want to make a website the premier destination for all weight loss information. If we can do this, we can be sure that we will attract a ton of website traffic and make lots of sales on our affiliate products.

So the first thing we need to do is, with different categories of information that relate to the niche market. For weight loss we can possibly come up with these main categories:

Weight Loss Categories

- Nutrition
- Exercises
- Equipment

After week, with our main categories we can further break down those categories into subcategories. These subcategories are going to tell us what we need to read our content about. So let's do that now:

ISBN: 978-0-9964087-2-1

Weight Loss Categories

- Nutrition
    - Dieting
    - Cooking
    - Healthy Foods
    - Weight Loss Pills
    - Weight Loss Shakes
- Exercises
    - Weight Lifting
    - Yoga
    - Pilates
    - Running
    - Swimming
    - Aerobics
- Equipment
    - Treadmills
    - Elliptical Trainers
    - Weights
    - Exercise Bikes
    - Rowers

You could potentially make even more subcategories in these, but for example purposes you can see how you can break down the categories into subcategories.

Once you have your list of subcategories you can start coming up with content ideas in the form of blog posts for each subcategory. If you do it correctly ability, with hundreds of ideas for content that you can create for your blog.

Here's an example of coming up with some content ideas for our first subcategory:

ISBN: 978-0-9964087-2-1

Weight Loss Categories

- Nutrition
  - Dieting
    - Blog Post #1: Does dieting really work?
    - Blog Post #2: The top 5 celebrity diets revealed
    - Blog Post #3: 10 things you can do to succeed with your diet
  - Cooking
    - Blog Post #1: Using low-fat cooking oils with your food
    - Blog Post #2: Five things you can do to start cooking healthy
    - Blog Post #3: Cooking accessories you must have if you plan on losing weight
  - Healthy Foods
    - Blog Post #1: Arugula - is it really is superfood?
    - Blog Post #2: Start your day with a vegetable shake if you want to lose weight
    - Blog Post #3: The top 10 fruits you should need for weight loss

You could potentially come up with hundreds of different types of blog post that you can create for each of your subcategories. The whole point of creating a blog posts to make them informative and helpful to the actual people who are going to be visiting your website.

Here is a list of some ideas to help you come up with different blog posts:

- Lists
- How to Guides
- Tips

- Current Events/Niche Related News
- Interviews
- Answer Questions
- Stories
- Charts, Graphs, Pictures
- Video Blog Posts
- Posted Research
- Case Studies
- Opinion Posts

Once you have your list of blog posts, you going to want to go in and ask you start writing them out. The blog posts need to be long enough so that they are informative and helpful to your website visitors. Don't make them too short because people won't be able to get any information out of them. Don't worry about how long they are, as longer blog posts tend to be more popular.

Creating Your Posting Schedule

You going to want to launch your informational blog with about 5 to 10 good blog posts. After that you going to need to place yourself on a Posting schedule. The more you post, the more content you'll have, and the more content you'll have the more visitors you'll be able to attract your blog. So you going to want to post as much and as often as possible in order to bring in the most amount of traffic.

Depending on your work and life schedule, you going to want to squeeze in as much posting as you can around your other obligations. At the very least do one post per day, but you should consider posting twice or even three times or more per day if possible in order to bring in a lot of traffic.

After you gotten a lot of posts onto your blog the next step is to start actually recommending affiliate products to your website visitors…

ISBN: 978-0-9964087-2-1

Part Four: Recommend Affiliate Products To Your Visitors

The next part of the process is to recommend affiliate products to your visitors. This is going to be how you're going to make your money. As people coming to your site and some your helpful content, it will be natural for them to want more information.

If you can strategically place your recommendations for products within your website and content, you can hook these people while they're looking for more information and provide them with a link to your affiliate product. If they purchase it you're going to make money. So let's talk about my favorite ways to recommend products as an affiliate...

Using Affiliate Banners

Affiliate banners are images, which are usually provided by the product vendor, that advertise the affiliate product for sale. These banners often eye-catching and use high-quality graphic images to entice website visitors to click on them. They usually promising type of big benefit that the visitor will receive for using the affiliate marketing product.

In order to get clicks to your affiliate links, you can post these banners onto your own informational blog website. The first thing you need to do is to find them on the product vendor's website. They will usually be under the affiliate resource section or similar area.

After that you need to post these images to your own website. The best place to put them is inside of the sidebar of the website. This way the image will appear on the home page and also on every blog post that you make. If you are familiar with how to add an image to the sidebar and Wordpress here's a link that will help you out: **http://www.youtube.com/watch?v=HbENt0YUf04**

ISBN: 978-0-9964087-2-1

Using a Resource Box

The next thing you can use to promote and recommend affiliate products to your website visitors called the resource box. The resource box is a bit of text that appears at the end of each and every blog post. A good resource box is going to tell them how purchasing the affiliate product will benefit them, and will also give a link to the affiliate product.

You are going to want to custom tailor the resource box to each individual blog post. So if your blog post is about a certain category of your niche market you want to make sure that the affiliate product you're promoting inside of the resource box is from the same category. For example, if your blog posts about nutrition and the weight loss niche, you'll probably want to post an affiliate product that promotes dieting or healthy eating inside of the resource box.

And just what should you right in the resource box? Well keeping with the same example let's see a resource box for this diet product:

> *If you've enjoyed this blog post and you're serious about losing weight then you need to check out amazing diet system!*
>
> *This system shows you how you can eat as much you want and still be able to lose 10 to 30 pounds within the next 60 days. If you like the sound of that please click the link below to check it out right now:*
>
> *[Your affiliate link]*

as you can see the resource box is short, sweet, and to the point. It doesn't need to be anything more than that in order for to work well. Just put a resource box at the end of every blog post

ISBN: 978-0-9964087-2-1

and you can rest assured that you're going to get a lot of traffic to your affiliate links.

The reason this works well is because the person will just have read a high quality content article about a certain subject. After people receive something of good quality, whether it be food or information, they're going to want more. Your resource box comes in at the right time and provides them with a link for them to check out more information. Once they click through, your product vendor takes over, and hopefully there able to close the sale.

Using Product Reviews

Product reviews are great way to get lots of traffic to your affiliate links. People will always seek out information on products that they are about to purchase. They especially want to find reviews of the product in order for them to get enough information to make an informed buying decision.

If you can write product reviews about popular products inside of your niche and post them to your blog people will be happy to read them. If you write them well, people will click through to your affiliate link and purchase the products.

Writing product reviews doesn't have to be hard either. All you need to do is write about all of the features and benefits that a product provides, and also mention any negatives that the customer could expect to experience when they purchase the product. As long as you cover all your bases, and give them a link to check out the product, you'll have a solid product review.

If you can do these things on your website you can rest assured that you're going to be recommending top-quality affiliate products your website visitors at the right time. But how do we get visitors over to our website to start with?

ISBN: 978-0-9964087-2-1

Part Five: Promote Your Informational Blog

the next step in the process of setting up your affiliate marketing business is a guy should get out there and start promoting your informational blog. Without driving traffic to your blog there won't be any sales in your affiliate account. So the more traffic you can get, the better. Now there are a ton of different ways to drive traffic on the Internet, some of them free and some of them cost money.

In this instance were going to use some of the top free methods of driving traffic to your informational blog. These methods work really well and will bring in highly targeted website visitors that will be likely to buy affiliate products from you. So let's get started right now...

Facebook

In case you haven't seen the movie, Facebook was created by college kid in his dorm room, and quickly grew to become a household name and a company of Internet and business legend. Now worth billions, this website is visited by nearly one out of every eight people on the entire planet.

Essentially, with Facebook you can post a profile. On this profile you can post pictures, videos, and update your status throughout the day. You can then network with others, and become "Facebook friends" and keep in contact with them through simple and clean interface.

ISBN: 978-0-9964087-2-1

Besides the social networking component, Facebook has a feature that is called "fan pages." With fan pages, a business, individual, website, or brand can create a Facebook presence that essentially functions the same way as a person's profile does. You can post related pictures, videos, and other information regarding your website.

People can then become a "fan" of your website and they can receive regular updates from you directly onto their own Facebook profile. This mechanism is very powerful, because you're able to access your audience directly on a platform which they use so often.

You can update your fan page saying that you posted an exciting new piece of content to your website, and it would automatically go out to all your fans. As your fans see this update in their profile, they can click on your link, and come to your website generating traffic for you.

So let's see how to use Facebook for traffic...

Step 1: Create A Facebook Fanpage

The first thing you would want to do is to create a personal profile for yourself if you don't already have one on Facebook. After you've created your personal profile, you can log into Facebook, and use your fan page creator to make your fan page.

Here's the link to do that:
https://www.facebook.com/pages/create.php/

When you create in your fan page, make sure that you post some initial content to it so that any new fans will have something to look at.

Step 2: Facebook Like Button Integration

ISBN: 978-0-9964087-2-1

The next step in need to take is to integrate the Facebook "like button" onto your website. When someone "likes" your website on Facebook, any updates that you send out through your fan page will also be sent to the people who "like" your website.

The easiest way to integrate a like button onto your website is to use the Facebook like widget:

https://developers.facebook.com/docs/reference/plugins/like/

It's pretty simple and straightforward to install your website, and if you run into any problems there are plenty of tutorials available for free online.

After you have done these two things your website is essentially fully integrated with Facebook, and you should begin a using this platform immediately to engage your audience directly. However, our social networking adventure is not complete. We must dive into the world of...

Twitter

Twitter is another huge social network. However it functions a little differently than Facebook. Where Facebook allows for users to have a profile with all types of videos, photos, and other information, Twitter does not. Instead, the draw of twitter is the ability to get short and quick status updates from people, brands, businesses, and websites that you're interested in. While Facebook has this feature too, Twitter was the first website to popularize this feature, known as "microblogging."

Now the reason why we want to use Twitter and Facebook, is because while some people use them both, others tend to focus solely on one network over the other. So since we want to spread

ISBN: 978-0-9964087-2-1

our traffic net far and wide to catch as many possible visitors, I suggest you integrate Twitter into your seven day traffic generation plan as well.

Because Twitter is a social network, they allow you to build friends, but on Twitter they're called followers.

How it works is as follows:

Each user has what is called a "tweet stream" where "tweets" from all the people that they are following come in, in real time. These tweets are limited to 140 characters, so they're often one to two sentence short blurbs about whatever it is the person is talking about.

For traffic purposes, if you have a Twitter following, and you want them to visit a specific link, you can write a short blurb and post the link to Twitter and some of your follower base will visit it. The larger your follower base is on Twitter, the more traffic you can generate from these types of tweets.

So let's see how to do it...

Step 1: Create Your Twitter Profile

The first thing you need to do is to create your own profile on Twitter. If you're trying to brand yourself, I suggest that you create a profile with your own name in it. If you want to brand your business or your website, make the business name or website name the name of your Twitter profile. By the way, all Twitter profiles have the @ symbol in front of them as well.

Creating your profile on Twitter is very straightforward and easy to do, and here's the link to get started:

https://twitter.com/signup

ISBN: 978-0-9964087-2-1

After you sign up to Twitter, and have created your profile, you're going to want to move onto the next step...

Step 2: Integrate Twitter On To Your Site

The next thing you need to do is to integrate your tweet stream directly onto your website. This is done by using the Twitter widget:

https://twitter.com/about/resources/widgets

The Twitter widget will show your tweet stream actively or your website, so any website visitors who have twitter accounts, can easily start following you on Twitter as well.

Step 3: Building A Twitter Following

Besides advertising your Twitter account on your webpage via the twitter widget, there some proactive things you can do to actually start building up your own follower base. You're probably going to want to do this, at least initially, because the more popular you appear on twitter, the more followers you can get.

Find Followers On Twitter Directories

Just like the phone directories of the old days, there are directories where people can post or twitter account information, and their interests, so that they can attract followers who have similar tastes as they do.

Here's a short list of the best twitter directories to use:

- http://www.twellow.com
- http://www.wefollow.com
- http://www.twitdir.com
- http://www.justtweetit.com
- http://www.tweetfind.com
- http://www.twittercounter.com
- http://www.twibs.com

ISBN: 978-0-9964087-2-1

Finding people in the twitter directories is pretty easy, and you can often search by people's profession, hobbies, and other interests.

If you want more followers you can also...

Find Followers On Niche Related Celebrity/Big Brand Twitter Accounts

You can find followers by browsing the list of the people who are following big brands are celebrities in your specific niche market. For instance, if you have a website about Ford Mustangs, and you want to find Twitter people to come to it, you could follow the official Ford Twitter account. After you follow them, you'll be able to see who else is following the official Ford account too. You can then follow all those people, and more than likely many of them will follow you back, building your own following.

Find Followers Using Twitter Search

Another simple yet effective way to find Twitter followers is to use http://search.twitter.com/

You can go here and just type in keywords related to your niche, and Twitter will find all of the people who have recently mentioned that keyword in one of their tweets. You can then follow these people, some of them will follow you back, building your Twitter following.

So this point you have established yourself on Twitter and Facebook, but we want to do even more.

We want to start...

ISBN: 978-0-9964087-2-1

Building Buzz And Getting Popular On Facebook and Twitter

There are some highly effective methods you can use to make yourself popular, get more Facebook friends, fans, likes, and Twitter followers. You can build buzz, get people talking about you, and in the process you'll build to generate a horde of traffic over to your website.

So let's see how to do this...

Step 1: Create Social Media Friendly Content

The first, and most obvious method, is to make sure that you're creating content that is friendly to social media type people. Social media users tend to be on the younger end of the age spectrum, and they enjoy easy-to-read content, that makes sense, and is informative. They also tend to like rich media like images and video, so if you're planning to build a big following there, make sure some of the content you create for your website falls into these categories.

Step 2: Run A Giveaway Contest

Another great way to get people talking about you on the social networks is to run a giveaway contest with a very desirable price. You want to make the prize related to your niche market in some way or you want to giveaway some highly desirable item like an iPhone or a new laptop. Either way make sure that it's a popular item that a lot of people are going to want. For instance if you're in the weight loss niche market, and a hot new weight loss DVD workout program this is come out, you can run a giveaway contest.

ISBN: 978-0-9964087-2-1

You can announce that people who "like" you on Facebook, or follow you on Twitter, will be entered into the drawing automatically. You'll notice a massive influx of new followers and Facebook fans and likes.

Now make sure you don't run the contest for longer than a month or so. This is because running a contest for too long will make people forget about it and the buzz will die down.

At the end of your giveaway contest, pick a winner, and proudly publicize you awarding them their price. Ask them to post pictures on their Facebook account, and tweet about them winning the prize. At the end of it, tell your social media followers and friends that there will be another contest soon so that they will keep up-to-date with your website.

Never underestimate the awesome traffic generation power giveaway contests!

Forums

Forum marketing is all about establishing a presence on niche related forums, and then using a signature link and in post references to drive traffic off of that forum and onto your website. The process is pretty simple and straightforward, but because you are required to participate in an active community it can require some time. However, the traffic you're getting from forums is going to be highly targeted to your niche market is going to be some of the best quality traffic you could find online.

So here's how to do it...

Step 1: Find Forums

First you need to find a set of niche related forums that you're going to actively be working in. Most good niches have tons of different forums, but like everything else there's often a small

ISBN: 978-0-9964087-2-1

handful of them that tend to attract the most traffic. The easiest place to find forums like this is to use a website called BigBoards – http://www.big-boards.com/

BigBoards is a forum directory that categorizes and lists forums by the amount of users that they have. You can access this website and quickly discover some of the biggest forums in your niche.

When you do find forums, make sure that they allow signature links that link to other websites. You can usually do this by reading their rules section or their FAQs section before registering.

Your signature link is a crucial component of the forum marketing process, and you don't want to waste time on a forum that doesn't allow them.

With that being said, pick 3 to 5 forums to work with and then move on to the next step…

Step 2: Participate In The Community

Now that you have your list of forums, the next thing you need to do is to start actively participating in the community. By participating, I mean that you need to post questions, answer questions, discuss, philosophize, pontificate, and generally communicate with others on the forum about your niche. The more you do this the better, and the more insight you put into your posts, the better reputation you will build for yourself.

Step 3: Promote With A Signature

I suggest that you spend a couple of weeks familiarizing yourself with the forum community, as well as building up a presence there. After that, you should introduce a signature link. Your

ISBN: 978-0-9964087-2-1

signature link is going to be a small blurb that appears at the end of each and every one of your forum posts. You can make this signature link back to your website.

Once you do this, each and every post on that forum has a small little advertisement for your website on it, and you can generate a ton of traffic this way.

Step 4: Form Strategic Alliances With Forum Owners

Besides signature traffic, you can also form strategic alliances with the owners of the form. So when you first join a forum, find out who owns it, and how you can contact them. Over time, after you have established yourself, you can contact these forum owners and tell them all about your business or website.

See if they are interested in letting you advertise or show banners on their forum. Or better yet, see if they will let you sponsor a forum. These things may cost you some money, but you need to remember, forums are the best place to find highly targeted traffic for your website.

ISBN:_978-0-9964087-2-1

Article Marketing

Article marketing is all about writing short informative articles, and posting them on many different article directories. An article directory website is a site that whose function is just what it sounds like. It stores a large amount of articles, categorized by subject matter, and allows its users to do some unique things with the articles.

People who use article directories can read the articles and learn information about a particular subject. They also can republish the articles on their website for free, as long as they give the author credit. This is usually done in the form of a small biography box, or "bio box" that tags along with the article when it is republished. Inside of his bio box you usually find links pointing back to the article author's website.

So as an article marketer, you want to create articles that are highly informative so that they get read by real people on the article directories. You also want to make the article so great that other webmasters want to republish them on their websites, so that you can get a link back to your website too. If you do this correctly the end result is that you get a ton of traffic. So let's dive into the actual step-by-step process of article marketing...

Step 1: Find Your Keyword & Research

The first thing you're going to need to do is find a search keyword to base your article around. You want to base your article around search keyword, because nearly all article directories rely almost exclusively on the search engines to bring traffic to their websites. So, if you do not target a specific search term your article won't get any views, and you won't generate any traffic to your website.

ISBN: 978-0-9964087-2-1

So the first thing you need to do is do keyword research to discover keywords that people are searching for. Here is a great link that shows you how to do that:

http://www.seosiren.com/how-to-find-low-competition-keywords-with-google-keyword-planner/

After you find keywords, you need to conduct some research on the actual subject you're going to be writing article about. If you have some pre-existing knowledge in the niche marketplace that you're targeting, it probably won't be very hard to come up with great article content. However if you don't, you should use the Internet and other resources to research your subject.

Step 2: Write Your Article

After you have a keyword handy and you have done your research, you need to actually sit down and create informative article based on the keyword. So let's use an example for the remainder of this step so that you can see just how easy this is to do.

Coming Up With A Good Article Title

The first thing you're going to need to do before writing your article, is to come up with a great article title. Your article title is going to be the first thing the visitors who are browsing article directory are going to see. A catchy title will gain you many more clicks, then a mediocre one. Therefore, you want to make sure that you spend a little time coming up with a great title.

The best way to come up with the title for your article, is to emulate the style of newspaper headlines. Newspaper headlines tend to be sensational and they try to grab the attention of the reader. They also tend to be short, sweet, and directly to the point. Finally, they may imply that there will be some type of benefit that will come from reading the article.

ISBN: 978-0-9964087-2-1

For this example let's say our keyword is "dwarf hamster care."

Here are some example article titles for that keyword:

> The Dwarf Hamster Care Secrets You Don't Know
>
> Simple Tips You Can Use to Give Awesome Dwarf Hamster Care
>
> Dwarf Hamster Care Doesn't Have To Be Hard Once You See This
>
> Dwarf Hamster Care the Easy Way

As you can see these titles are pretty good and they will probably get a lot of clicks and bring readers to our article. Also you'll notice that the titles include the search keyword term that were targeting as well.

The Simple Article Template That Works

The next step in creating your article is actually sit down and write it. Now, if you've never written an article before, this can seem like a daunting task but don't worry. I'm going to show you an easy to use article template, so that you will have no trouble creating the article.

The template for the article is as follows, tell them what you're about to tell them, tell them, then tell them what you told them. So in the first paragraph, make an introduction where you talk about the general subject that the article is going to be about. Then after that, you write 2 to 4 paragraphs that give the actual details on your article subject. Finally, in the last paragraph you recap, and you go over what you just said.

To get even more detailed here's a simple outline you can follow to use this template:

- introductory paragraph

ISBN: 978-0-9964087-2-1

    - sentence number one: introduce the subject
    - sentence number two: talk about the benefits they will get after reading the article
    - sentence number three: talk about the subject matter of your article
    - sentence number four: tell them what you're about to tell them inside of the article
- paragraph number 1, 2, 3, and 4
    - sentence number one: introduce the main idea of paragraph
    - sentence number two: supporting detail of the main idea
    - sentence number three: supporting detail of the main idea
    - sentence number four: supporting detail of the main ideas
    - sentence number five: conclude paragraph in transition to next paragraph
- closing paragraph
    - sentence number one: recap the main idea from paragraph 1
    - sentence number two: recap the main idea from paragraph 2
    - sentence number three: recap the main idea from paragraph 3
    - sentence number four: recap the benefit they will receive the results they can expect from following the advice article

An article written this template follows a logical consistent flow, is easy-to-read, and actually can be informative as long as you what you write is actually good. When you're writing articles for

ISBN:_978-0-9964087-2-1

article marketing you want to make them at least 500 words or more, but you don't need to make them over 1500 or so words.

Step 3: Create Your Bio

The next step is to create your bio box. Your bio box is a short little blurb that comes at the end of the article where you can talk a little bit about yourself, and guide the reader of your article to visit your webpage. With that being said the best way to create a bio is to keep it simple. All you need to do is write a sentence or two about yourself and why you have expertise in the subject matter of the article. Then simply say if you want more information "check out my website" or something to that effect.

Step 4: Submit Your Article

The next thing to do is to submit your article to the article directories. There are many article directories to choose from online, but about 20% of them get about 80% of all traffic that's out there looking for articles. So you should probably focus your efforts on these article directories.

Here's a short list of the top 10 recommended article directories to submit your article to:

- http://www.ehow.com/ - (How To Articles)
- http://www.squidoo.com/
- http://www.ezinearticles.com/
- http://www.hubpages.com/
- http://www.articlesbase.com/
- http://www.buzzle.com/
- http://www.apsense.com/
- http://www.goarticles.com/
- http://www.pubarticles.com/ - (How To Articles)
- http://www.articlesnatch.com/

ISBN: 978-0-9964087-2-1

A Word On Unique Content

Now at this point you may be wondering whether or not you need to create a separate article for each article directory plan you on submitting to, or can you submit the same article to multiple directories. Well we used to be able to submit the same article with little to no changes to multiple directories and not suffer any penalties.

However, due to new updates in Google's algorithms this is no longer recommended. Instead, you should create a unique keyword targeted article for each separate article directory you plan on submitting to. This way you get the maximum benefit that you can from the article marketing efforts.

ISBN: 978-0-9964087-2-1

Conclusion

Hopefully this guide has given you a great overview on how to do affiliate marketing correctly. There is no doubt that affiliate marketing is here to stay. It is not a fad or passing trend, so you need to take action on this strategy starting right now.

Nothing happens without Action, so start implementing today. I mean right now this very moment, do at least one thing towards setting up in affiliate marketing business. Even if it's as small as just registering your domain, or if it is as complex to planning out an entire affiliate marketing strategy. Do something right now!

Keep working one step a time and complete each task. With consistent daily activity you will succeed in your online business.

Do not get distracted by shiny objects and keep focus in whatever task you undertake and complete it before you go to next task.

I look forward to hearing your affiliate marketing success story,

-VJ Shah

ISBN: 978-0-9964087-2-1

Resources:

Domain Registration & Hosting:

GoDaddy.com

Domainsandprofit.com

Namecheap.com

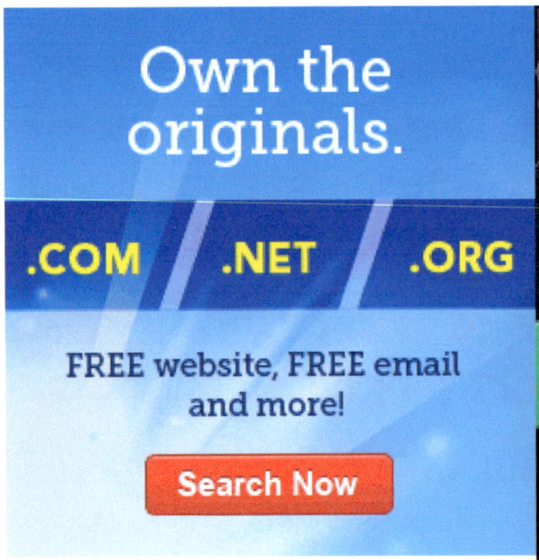

Autoresponders:

Gogvo.com

http://GetResponse.com

Aweber.com

Click The Banner Below To Join FREE & Build Your List of Subscribers.

ISBN: 978-0-9964087-2-1

Made in the USA
Las Vegas, NV
07 November 2026

57650031R00026